CREATION STORIES

BY VIRGINIA LOH-HAGAN

People have been telling stories since the beginning of time. This series focuses on stories found across cultures. You may have heard these stories from your parents or grandparents. Or you may have told one yourself around a campfire. Stories explain the world around us. They inspire. They motivate. They even scare! We tell stories to share our history.

45th Parallel Press

Published in the United States of America by Cherry Lake Publishing
Ann Arbor, Michigan
www.cherrylakepublishing.com

Reading Adviser: Marla Conn MS, Ed., Literacy specialist, Read-Ability, Inc.
Book Designer: Jen Wahi

Photo Credits: ©worradirek/Shutterstock.com, 5; ©AXL/Shutterstock.com, 7; ©Darkfoxelixir/Shutterstock.com, 8;
©iofoto/Shutterstock.com, 11; ©Kirk Geisler/Shutterstock.com, 13; ©My Generations Art/Shutterstock.com, 14; ©ifong/
Shutterstock.com, 17; © Sarah Fields Photography/Shutterstock.com, 19; © WIRACHAIPHOTO/Shutterstock.com, 21;
©Raul H/Shutterstock.com, 23; © Harvepino/Shutterstock.com, 25; © frankie's/Shutterstock.com, 27; ©Thoom/
Shutterstock.com, 28; ©Maridav/Shutterstock.com, cover and interior; Various grunge/texture patterns throughout
courtesy of Shutterstock.com

45th Parallel Press is an imprint of Cherry Lake Publishing.

Library of Congress Cataloging-in-Publication Data

Names: Loh-Hagan, Virginia, author.
Title: Creation stories / by Virginia Loh-Hagan.
Description: Ann Arbor : Cherry Lake Publishing, 2019. | Series: Stone circle
   stories: culture and folktales | Includes bibliographical references and
   index.
Identifiers: LCCN 2018035179| ISBN 9781534143524 (hardcover) | ISBN
   9781534141285 (pdf) | ISBN 9781534140080 (pbk.) | ISBN 9781534142480
   (hosted ebook)
Subjects: LCSH: Creation--Mythology--Juvenile literature..
Classification: LCC BL325.C7 L59 2019 | DDC 202/.4--dc23
LC record available at https://lccn.loc.gov/2018035179

Printed in the United States of America
Corporate Graphics

ABOUT THE AUTHOR:

Dr. Virginia Loh-Hagan is an author, university professor, and former classroom teacher. She creates stories about everything and everyone. She lives in San Diego with her very tall husband and very naughty dogs. To learn more about her, visit www.virginialoh.com.

TABLE OF CONTENTS

CREATION STORIES

What are creation stories?
How are they different from pourquoi stories?

Most cultures have **creation stories**. These are special stories. They explain how the world was formed. They explain where people came from. They explain how animals came to be. They try to explain the unknown. They're not based on science. They're based on people's ideas and beliefs.

Creation stories are different from **pourquoi** stories. Pourquoi is a French word. It means "why." Pourquoi stories explain why something is the way it is. An example is why dogs bark.

All religions have a creation story.
Some may have creator gods.

Creation stories focus on the creation of the world. Pourquoi stories explain everything in the world. Both types of stories are fun to read.

CHAPTER 1

THE WOMAN WHO FELL FROM THE SKY

Who are the Sky People?
How did the Sky Woman fall?
How was the world created?

The Iroquois and Huron are Native Americans. They're from the northeastern part of the United States. They have a creation story about the Sky Woman.

In the beginning, the Sky People lived in a world above the sky. They lived on an island. They floated in the sky. There was a tree in the middle of the island.

The Sky Woman is also called Ataensic.

The tree gave light. No one was ever sad. No one ever died. No one was ever born.

The Sky Woman became **pregnant**. Pregnant means having a baby inside. The Sky Woman told her husband. Her husband got mad. He tore up the tree. He made a hole in the island. He pushed the Sky Woman down the hole.

The Sky Woman fell. As she was falling, ducks flew under her. They tried to slow her down. They carried her on their backs. The Sky Woman landed in water. She didn't see any land. A turtle rose from the water. The turtle let the Sky Woman rest on its back.

In some stories, the Sky Mother is called Grandmother Moon.

SPOTLIGHT BIOGRAPHY

Georges Lemaître was a priest, soldier, and scientist. He lived from 1894 to 1966. He was born in Belgium. He got a doctorate at the Massachusetts Institute of Technology. He studied other scientists. He did a lot of math. He learned the universe was growing in the same way in all directions. He believed the universe came from a tiny point. He called it a "cosmic egg." He believed the egg exploded at the time of creation. At first, his ideas weren't popular. Many people disagreed with him. But then he became a star. Today, he's known as the "father of the big bang theory." Theory means idea. The big bang theory explains how the universe began. It says the universe started with a hot, thick glob. Then, there was a big blast. This happened billions of years ago. The glob blew up and expanded. All matter and energy including space and time burst forth. Galaxies formed and moved away. They moved in all directions.

A toad appeared. It opened its mouth. There was mud in its mouth. The Sky Woman spread the mud on the turtle's back. The mud grew and grew. It became North America. The Sky Woman stepped onto the land.

The Sky Woman gave birth. She had twins. She had two sons. One son was good. One son was bad.

The good son shaped the sky. He made the sun. He made the moon. He made the stars. He made the mountains. He made rivers. He made plants. He made animals. He made humans. He made summer.

The bad son tried to ruin his brother. He made darkness. He wanted to drive the sun from the sky. He made monsters. He made storms. He made winter.

They had a war. The good brother won. He kicked the bad brother out of earth. The bad brother became the king of the underworld. Underworld is where dead people live. The bad brother was angry. His anger became volcanoes.

In some stories, the Sky Woman had a daughter. The daughter gave birth to sons.

CHAPTER 2

SILVER FOX AND COYOTE

What are Silver Fox and Coyote like?
How did they create the world?

Silver Fox was a creator god. He appears in stories from Northern California **tribes**. Tribes are groups of Native Americans. Silver Fox worked with Coyote. They created the world. Silver Fox was wiser. He liked to make things. Coyote was a **trickster**. Tricksters play tricks. Coyote liked to destroy things. He was lazy.

In the beginning, there was no earth. There was only water. Silver Fox and Coyote lived above the sky. Silver Fox got annoyed with Coyote. He sent him out to get wood. While he was gone, Silver Fox made a hole in the

In some stories, Silver Fox is female.

world. He looked down. He saw the sea. He didn't tell Coyote.

Coyote left again. Silver Fox climbed down the hole. He landed in the water. He made a small island for himself.

Coyote came back. He was lonely. He looked for Silver Fox. He found the hole. He saw Silver Fox on his island. He yelled down, "Can I join you?"

I jam out to "What Does the Fox Say?" on repeat.

In some stories, Silver Fox and Coyote make the world by singing and dancing.

Silver Fox said, "This island isn't big enough for the both of us."

Coyote said, "I'm coming anyway." He dropped down.

Silver Fox and Coyote tried to sleep. There wasn't enough room. So, Silver Fox made the island bigger. At last, they could sleep. They were hungry. There wasn't enough room to hunt. Silver Fox made the island bigger. At last, they could eat.

FAST-FORWARD TO MODERN TIMES

The Church of the Flying Spaghetti Monster started in 2005. It was started by Bobby Henderson. Henderson studied science. He was against public schools teaching intelligent design. Intelligent design is the idea of one being creating the world. Henderson made a joke. He said that if schools taught intelligent design, then they should also teach Pastafarianism. Pastafarianism is the belief that the Flying Spaghetti Monster (FSM) created the world. One day, the FSM separated water from the heavens. But then it grew tired of swimming and flying. So it made land. The FSM kept making more land and more water. The FSM did this because it kept forgetting that it had already made land and water. FSM also made the stars, sun, moon, and small people.

Silver Fox was annoyed with Coyote. He wanted more room away from Coyote. He made a house. He dressed up. He danced. He moved his feet. He pushed the land out in all directions.

He told Coyote to run around the edge of the earth. He wanted to see how large the land was. Coyote did this. Each time, it took Coyote longer and longer to return home. The land grew very large. Coyote came home tired. He was too tired to do his tricks.

While Coyote was away, Silver Fox could work. He made trees. He made rivers. He made animals. He made people.

In some stories, Coyote plucks feathers from a bird. The feathers turn into people.

CHAPTER 3

WAKEA AND PAPA

Who are Wakea and Papa?
How did they make the world?
Who are their children?

Hawaii is in the Pacific Ocean. It's a group of islands. It has several creation stories. The story of Wakea and Papa is the most popular. There are several versions.

In the beginning, there was only darkness. Papa was the goddess of darkness. She ruled the underworld. She was a creator goddess. She had the power to give life. She had the power to heal.

Papa is short for Papahanaumoku. In some stories, she's responsible for making the Hawaiian islands.

Then, there was light. The light was made by Wakea. Wakea was the Sky Father. He was the god of light. He was the god of the heavens. He also was a creator god.

Wakea and Papa got married. Papa became the Earth Mother. She had a baby boy. But the baby died. He was born without arms or legs. Wakea and Papa were sad.

CROSS-CULTURAL CONNECTION

The story of Pan Ku comes from China. Long ago, sky and earth were one. The entire world was in an egg. Pan Ku was in the egg. He was asleep. He grew taller each day. He grew for 18,000 years. He finally woke up. He stretched. He pushed apart the egg. He released the world. Lighter things floated to the sky. Heavier things dropped to the earth. Pan Ku kept sky and earth apart. He kept growing. He did this for another 18,000 years. The sky and earth grew farther apart. Then, Pan Ku fell apart. His arms and legs became the mountains. His blood became rivers. His sweat became rain. His breath became wind. His voice became thunder. His eyes became the sun and moon. His hair became plants. His veins became roads. His teeth and bones became rocks. His muscles became soil. The bugs living on his body became humans.

They buried their baby in a garden. A plant grew over his body. The plant made a magical gourd. Gourds are large fruits. Wakea and Papa thought the gourd was their son. They named him Haloa.

Wakea took the gourd. He cut it up. He threw the pieces up. The top formed the sky. The meat of the fruit became the sun. The seeds became the moon and stars. The juices became rain and clouds. The skin became the land and seas.

Together, Wakea and Papa made light and dark. They made earth and sky. They made good and evil. They

In some stories, Haloa became a taro plant. Many Hawaiians eat taro.

I may be hairy and a little odd looking, but I'm delicious when cooked!

represent balance. They're the first parents of all life. Papa planted seeds on her land. Wakea gave the sun, rain, and dirt. This made the plants grow.

Wakea and Papa had other children. Some were coral, fish, seaweed, trees, birds, animals, and humans. They told their children to pass down their story. They told their children to respect nature.

The children of Wakea became chiefs.

KAMEHAMEHA
THE GREAT

CHAPTER 4

MBORI

Who are Mbori and his sons?
What was in the canoe?
How was the world created?

People were taken from Africa. They were sold into **slavery**. Slavery is the owning of humans to do free work. The United States participated in the slave trade. This was a bad time in history. Many of the slaves came from the Congo area. Congo is a country in Africa. When people came, they brought their stories.

Mbori was a Congo creator god. He was powerful. He had all the knowledge in the world. He made earth. He made fire. He made air. He made water. He made animals. He made humans. He put all these things in a **canoe**. Canoes are small boats.

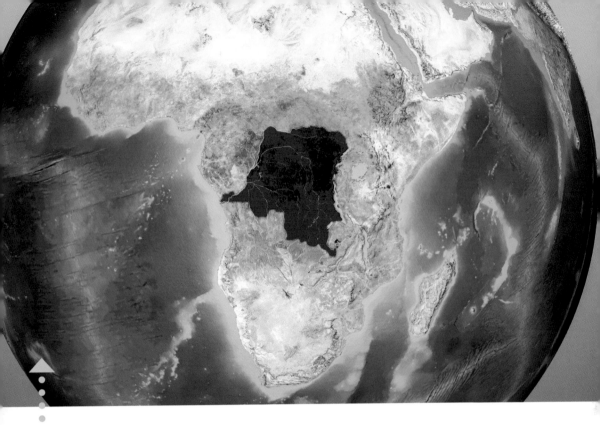

Congo is the second-largest country in Africa.

Mbori sealed up the canoe. He left a hole. He plugged the hole with wax. He put special juice over the wax. The juice made a small stain in the wood.

Mbori was dying. He called out to his **messenger**. Messengers send notes. Mbori said, "Messenger, please bring my sons here. I need to see them."

The messenger did as he was told. He went to each of the sons' homes. Mbori's sons were Sun, Moon, Night, Stars, and Cold. The messenger told each son, "Come with me. Your father needs you."

The messenger liked Sun the best. He pulled Sun aside. He said, "I'll tell you a secret. Look for a stain."

Sun asked, "What does that mean?"

The messenger said, "You'll find out soon."

The sons went to Mbori. Mbori said, "Sons, I'm dying. You need to open the canoe. Whoever opens it will rule the world. Everything will spin around him."

Mbori is also called Bapaizegino or Mboli.

Each son tried. Each son failed. Then Sun remembered what the messenger told him. He tried again. He found the stain. He saw the wax plug. He became hot. He melted the wax. He opened the hole. All the living things came out. This was how the world was formed.

Many creation stories feature the sun.

DID YOU KNOW?

> Creation stories are also called cosmological stories. Cosmology is a science. It's the study of the beginnings of the universe. The universe is all matter and space. It includes planets and stars.

> A creation story from Australia features a rainbow snake. The world was sleeping. The rainbow snake was the first to wake up. It woke the frogs. It tickled the frogs. The frogs laughed out water. The water flowed. It made plants. It woke up other animals. Animals that followed the snake's rules became human. Animals that broke laws became rocks.

> Mbombo is an African creator god. First, he threw up the sun. Then, he threw up the moon, stars, animals, plants, and humans.

> Purusha is from Hindu stories. He killed himself to create the world. Part of him became butter. Gods used the butter to create animals. They cut up his body parts to form the rest of the world.

CHALLENGE:

WRITE YOUR OWN TALE

BEFORE YOU WRITE:

❯ Read other creation stories. Read stories from different cultures. Use these stories as models.

❯ Decide the topic of your creation story. Think of things in nature. Examples are animals, the moon, the sun, and stars.

❯ Brainstorm how things came to be. Make a list of ideas.

❯ Explain why things came to be. Make a list of ideas.

❯ Consider whether or not to include a creator god.

AS YOU WRITE:

❯ Start with the line: "In the beginning …" Set the scene for how things were before the earth was formed.

❯ Describe the setting. Tell when and where the story takes place.

❯ Describe the characters.

❯ Describe the problem.

❯ Explain how a character solves the problem. Describe a series of events. Have the character make mistakes and learn from them.

❯ End the story describing the change.

AFTER YOU WRITE:

❯ Proofread and edit your creation story.

❯ Add interesting details as needed. Use creative language.

❯ Make sure your creation story explains something. Does it explain how things came to be? Does it explain why certain things act in a certain way? Does it explain how a certain thing looks?

❯ Host a story-sharing event. Read your creation story out loud.

❯ Think about creating your own world. This is what fantasy writers do.

CONSIDER THIS!

TAKE A POSITION! Learn more about the big bang theory. Learn more about intelligent design. Did the universe start with a bang? Or has the universe always existed? Cultures create myths to explain the creation of the world. Science also has ideas about how the world started. What do you believe and why? Argue your point with reasons and evidence.

SAY WHAT? Research creationism. Research evolution. Explain each one. Explain how they're the same. Explain how they're different.

THINK ABOUT IT! Read the 45th Parallel Press series about Greek and Norse myths. How did the Greek and Norse people explain the creation of the world? How did they explain nature? How did they explain people? Why are myths important? What is the purpose of myths?

LEARN MORE!

Goble, Paul. *The Earth Made New: Plains Indian Stories of Creation*. Bloomington, IN: World Wisdom, Inc., 2009.

Hamilton, Martha, and Mitch Weiss. *How & Why Stories*. Little Rock, AR: August House Publishers, 1999.

Mayo, Margaret. *When the World Was Young: Creation and Pourquoi Tales*. New York: Simon & Schuster Books for Young Readers, 1996.

GLOSSARY

canoe (kuh-NOOH) a small boat with pointed ends that needs paddles to move

creation stories (kree-AY-shuhn STOR-eez) special stories that explain how the world was formed

gourd (GORD) large fruit with a hard rind or skin

messenger (MES-uhn-jur) a person whose job is to deliver messages or notes

pourquoi (por-QWAH) French word for "why"

pregnant (PREG-nuhnt) having a baby growing inside

slavery (SLAY-vur-ee) the owning of humans to do work

tribes (TRYBZ) groups of people

trickster (TRIK-ster) a character that plays tricks

underworld (UHN-dur-wurld) the place under the world where dead people live

INDEX